EXPERIENCES WITH RABBITS

JOAN K. FAYAS

authorHOUSE®

AuthorHouse™
1663 Liberty Drive
Bloomington, IN 47403
www.authorhouse.com
Phone: 1-800-839-8640

First published by AuthorHouse 7/31/2009

ISBN: 978-1-4490-0322-7 (sc)

Printed in the United States of America
Bloomington, Indiana

This book is printed on acid-free paper.

TABLE OF CONTENTS

1

THE BEGINNING

The first rabbits we had were called New Zealands, I was told. They were pure white with black spots and some looked like they had mustaches. They were so adorable! Then we decided to buy a male and female to breed and they were called "Mustache and Muffin. At the time, we were so new at this business and the guy who sold them to us said they were male and female, but he wrong and we got two males. We began to collect different rabbits. **We bought them from the flea markets in alabama and also saw an ad in the paper of rabbits for sale. We went to see what the lady had and got one that looked like a squirrel (male) and one the lady said was a female that was gray and really pretty, so we thought they would breed well. We called them squirrel and Pearl, they were both dwarf rabbits that stayed small. You could tell by their ears (short) that they would remain little. WE didn't understand why they didn't produce at all, and squirrel would go arould to all the other females we had and seemed to be producing quite a bit. Once again we found out that Pearl was also a male and we were led wrong. We didn't realize at the time, how fast they multiplied, until we started having 20-30 rabbits easily.**

2

🐰

MOTHERS AND BABIES

We would put a fenced yard out during the day to let them play and romp around, eat grass, and excercise, until some dogs came and trampled down the fence and the rabbits ran out all over the neighborhood. We did lose alot of rabbits then. We had to go with a net to chase them and try to net them, but it i is no easy job, rabbits are fast and are gone before you can lower the net. When you catch them, you are lucky....

After a good day of trying to get them so you can put them back in the pen, you are pretty worn out, and have had your exercise for the day..

We had really nice cages we made for them that even has a little house on the end just for the mothers who are having babies.You put their hay in it and the mothers add their fur to make a nest for their new arrivals. If their were more mothers to have babies at the same time, we have wooden boxes upside down for them as well and they can be just as comfortable in them to deliver their babies. We would have many learning experiences as time went on. We learned to keep the mothers by theirselves before they are about to deliver. One reason, was that she didn't like feeding them if she had other company. She would stay by the other females and not attend to her babies to feed. We had a few die this way, not getting fed.. We also had a mother die, and the babies were left for us to have to force feed to live. It's a SAD EXPERIENCE, BUT ONE YOU HAVE TO TRY TO TAKE CHARGE OF AND HOPE YOU CAN KEEP THE BABIES ALIVE. It can be very traumatic. I know those we lost our hearts went with them. We felt like they were a part of us. You are trying to keep them alive, but sometimes you don't succeed.

Make sure when you have a rabbit cage, that the wiring is very tiny and as small as you can get and as high up in the air as you can bacause a raccoon, possum,. cat, or rat can reach up in there with their claws and pull a babies foot through the hole and chew if off. We had this happen to us and it isn't a pretty sight to see. That was also an experience you want to avoid, it hurts you deeply. Not only can that happen, but a rat can get through small wire and he will also eat the babies, or chew them up. Always remember the old saying, and it's true "Rabbits are the first on the food chain." That means they are the first prey to die.

Mothers can produce rabbits about every 30 days, so we see now why they say they multiply so fast. It's not nine months like us, every 30 days.

One of our best producing females is a brownish, red color doe we call "Cinny" Her real name is cinnamon. She breeds every 30 days, it seems like. You need to try to get them to breed more in the winter, because summer is too hard on them in the heat.We don't even like our rabbits penned up in the summer because of too much heat. We let them loose in our fenced back yard, With plenty of places, to hide as well as food and plenty of water.

3

MORE RABBITS

In the first two years of having rabbits, we had a white rabbit with black dots all over. Her name was "Eight ball." She was a good producer, but she grew real big and one night she tried to back down a raccoon in the back yard. We had to chase the raccoon out because he kept getting closer to her and we didn't want her killed. She had alot of babies with black mustaches and white with black dots.

We have had several different rabbits, different types and different colors. Each of them we have, We always find a name for. They reminded us of someone or something

We had a white rabbit, called "Sprint." I named him that because when he was a baby, he was double fast. He was a pure white rabbit with huge dark eyes, and then we had a white rabbit with black on him and real pretty blue eyes, which we called "Blue." It is hard to keep males together because they are so territorial and they fight to their death or scratch each others eyelids or eyes. They want all the female rabbits to themselves. White rabbits can have a problem… They can easily be seen. Therefore, they will get caught by their predators faster than others. From what I have seen, though, they seem to be the toughest around the predators.

A few years ago, we picked up our first Lionshead. This is a very special breed out of Begium. They have beautiful soft fur and between their ears, on top of their head they have like a fur top that stands up. Reminds you of someone that had their hair punk on top, like it was teased. The first one we got was a pure white one with pink/red eyes that had the softest fur and looked like an angel. That is what we called it, "Angel." We again, were told that Angel was a female, but wasn't, but we kept it's name anyway. He cost $35.00 when we got him, then we got 3 more lionsheads later. One was a male and the other a female with brown furs and we called them "Sonny and Cher." The male looked like a Sonny for some reason, hence, comes Cher.. The other lionshead we got that day was a gray female we call "Sammy." Each of these cost $35.00 when we got them, except Sonny and Cher cost $40.00 each. They weren't cheap like $10.00. The lionsheads are worth it to me. The only problem we had was our babies got eaten. The rat did it, which greatly upset us...

4

TILTHEAD AND THUMPERS

We got a lop ear rabbit with light brown and white and it got the disease called "Tilt head." It has to do with the inner ear and they end up with a head that tilts to one side. They act pretty normal but they go around in circles like they are dizzy. We had the first tilthead rabbit, called "Thumper." He died, so we bought another one and called him the same cause he looked just like him, and we forgot that he came from the same family, and ended up with tilthead and died. This Thumper did not seem unhappy, and even though he ran around in circles, and was tilted, he seemed to be content even with his bunny friends. It was a real tragedy for us, because we left him alone to get his exercize and air, and he got eaten alive from his bottom parts to his stomach. It was the worst thing I ever saw.

5

🐰

PREDATORS

The reddish-orange colored cat was seen by my husband under the house. He fell asleep there, right next to the dead babies bodies which he had killed. My husband couldn't get him at the time.

Then we had another incident, where the cat was running trying hard to get out of our fenced yard, and unbelievably he jumped 8 ft. up in the air and over the top of a piece of tin that is nailed to the top of a 6ft. fence. We couldn't believe that cats could jump that high, but he saw it with his own eyes. We also found out that cats are one of the toughest predators. They can jump on prey with 4 feet and bite them in the throat, suffocate them and they die.

Now as we continue, let's talk about raccoons. We have had twelve raccoons come in the yard. How they got in the fenced yard is unknown, and they kill and eat the rabbits. Now the oppossums we have had in here, about 28, at different times, usually just pick up the leftovers of the dead bunnies after they have been killed or eaten. We relocate them when we catch them in a trap. They are brought by a pond about 2 miles away and let go. We are beginning to think that having rabbits can become a losing battle, being number 1 on the food chain to be killed or eaten makes us wonder if its all worth while.

6

Digging And Neighbors

Rabbits whether male or female, it seems, like to dig... They will try to dig their way out of a fence and most of the time succeed. Some of the neighbors don't want them around because they dig holes in their yards or eat their gardens, which is understandable. Most of the neighbors we find really like and enjoy them around. One woman told me she enjoys watching them, as we do. You can have quite a bit of entertainment watching them, they are funny and cute. If it takes us to patch up a few holes, it gets done, but some people like their animals and we like ours.

7

SOME FOOD FOR US

Now, speaking of the chow we have found that rabbits are a lot like us in the manner of different tastes. Some like one thing and some like another, but they, like us, love to eat!!

Besides their pellets and romaine lettuce, they seem to love saltine crackers, bread,white or wheat, corn, carrots, bananas, pears, and what not. They eat pretty many things. We found out they eat branches of willow trees, and popcorn tree leafs. They like a lot so you just have to try different things to see, some things you will be surprised at. MY RABBITS Never seemed to like alfalfa. They like the treats you can get at the store. Its a log type deal with vitamins in it. We have been told that lettuce isn't too good as it causes diarhea. Although we give it to them, sometimes, we try different things sometimes to test them, see if they like it.

8

🐰

Our Rabbits Now

We picked up a rabbit at the Dothan flea market and he was different. He has dark brown with tan and white markings and big ears. He has the big ears, but seems to be staying a smalle size. He's adorable and we all played with him since we brought him home. We call him "Rootbeer." He looks like a rootbeer float. Recently he got a female pregnant and the babies are adorable. One is ran and white, one is pure gold color and one is his image, baby Rootbeer. He must have impregnated all the females here. I'm sure we will be seeing all different kinds of babies come next. I'm sure their will be quite a variety...

One of the mothers, I think it may be Red, had a batch, and possiblely Blackie the other mother. The other babies are black with a white nose, one black with one white left paw which I call southpaw. There is one black with white in different areas,there is a gray Lionhead baby with beautiful gray and silver fur, we believe must be Sammy's baby. .We have a baby SONNY, lionshead, and a white one with a dirty colored nose. We have the lionshead Sammy I mentioned, who is a beautiful gray and white rabbit. Then their is the buck rabbit that is huge, like a dog, and we call him Jake. He is white and has black spots and fur like a lionshead in the middle of his head. He is also a lop ears. We had heard that a buck would chase a cat or another animal away but we only see Jake chase our rabbits for execise and because they bother him. We watch him because he is so much bigger than the others and he could hurt them by accident if he trampled on them. If he goes after a predator, it is yet to be seen... When we got Jake, we also bought a little dwarf rabbit, a baby, we called "Licorice, because being black and white , it was adorable and looked like a good name for her. She was gone when we woke up the next morning, we don't know if a cat got her or another predator. We never found any fur or signs of her again. Just when you start getting close, this is what you deal with, tragedy.. Sometimes you wonder if you should be in this business. When you see a rabbit, like I did this morning, who is carrying hay in his mouth and running you know they are pregnant and due for babies any day. We will have a litter soon. Our biggest litter, i beleve we had, was from Cinnamon who had 9 babies at a time.

9

THE NEIGHBORS

We have friends that live down the street, have rabbits, I guess we got them into rabbits, Kevin and Michelle Rowland. We gave them a bunch of rabbits to start and then they bought some for themselves. They also bought a lionshead too. We are always checking with each other to see how things are going. We have to watch for the predators, and we always get suggestions from each other on different matters that arise with the rabbits. They have put aside a room, like a florida room for the rabbits to go in, so it's different. There is also a pond on the side of their house which the rabbits can visit. Our house in back has alot of driftwood for the rabbits to hide under, and it is fenced in. Some of our other neighbors that we gave rabbits to won't tell us when our rabbits get out and go in their yard. It sort of gets upsetting for me because then we don't know if a predator got them or not. Most neighbors are friendly but we notice that this neighborhood has a lot to be desired. There are some nice people and some are neighbors you can live without. There is a couple across the street that hate everything and are always complaining about something or other. They called in about our rabbits, but it's okay when their 3 dogs bark all day and night and yip. Everyone has to put up with their noise, and not have a life. They really need to get a life for themselves. Most people like to watch the rabbits, and never complain. As far as the rabbits, they are nice because they don't ever talk back, they don't ask of you more than you can give, only they like to be pet, unless they have been in the wild and they need love. They run away if they get used to being in the wild! They are touchy, if they think you are nearing them like a predator..oMy rabbits like music. They sit and listen and their ears go up. The rabbits we have brought in the house like to watch t.v., and like it. They never complain and eat pretty much of the food you give them.

10.

A New Batch And New Ones Rescued

Every time we get a new batch of rabbits, I go crazy and want more. I don't even think about all of them multipling...

Jake was getting too lonesome. We had to put him inthe pen because the little rabbits were running around and some of the bigger rabbits picked on himand tore his fur up. So, we went to Troy Alabama and got a female . A big huge rabbit like Jake from Jimmy, the guy we buy some from. We call her Jackie and she is white and black spots but more black in her than Jake. They love each other- maybe we will get another litter soon from them.

Meanwhile, all these little babies are popping up out from under the shed and under the house and are adorable. There is a tan one, a rabbit like Rootbeer, but he looks as if he were sprayed cause he got white and brown and it looks sprayed on... There are little black ones with tan ears, a set of twins, and I'm sure there will be more popping out again, since Rootbeer is so spoiled by females. Ha! Ha!

We will be going to Dothan, tommorow so guess who will return with bunnies, if there are ones we want.

11

Bunny Babies Are Comming Out All Over Back Yard, And Rudy The Rooster

We returned Saturday arternoon and belive it or not, with no rabbits. Maybe, it was a good thing because the next day when I looked outside there were baby bunnies comming out all over the back yard. There were about 2-3 brown and white ones, and 3 brown ones. Their colors are really pretty, and a little tan one. In the front yard, I saw one of my lionsheads babies. There are 2 more over the neighbors and the mother, Sammy. They are gorgeous gray and white...

Today, we went to get the rabbits feed at the feed store and there was a pretty rooster there. Sandy, the owner, said we could have him, so we brought him home. We call him "Rudy." We thought we lost him tonight because we couldn't find him... There he was, hiding up under my grill on the deck.. It was really funny when I found him there. I had the biggest laugh, right where you never expect him..

The rabbits were really shocked to come face to face with Rudy the rooster. They weren't expecting him. They wanted to fight but Rootbeer, who is the bossiest rabbit here, finally backed down One of the black and white bunnies called "Southpaw," doesn't back down as much so we will have to watch them.

There is also a freeze warning for tonight here. I thought we had better try to catch some of the babies and put them in the cage with Lollypop and Licorice so they could be warm... There's hay all over in there and they could cuddle together, to keep warm. We only got three, so hopefully the other ones will go into the ground holes they made. They can also go under the house. I don't know what Rudy will do because he just came today and he doesn't know the yard good yet. Maybe, he will stay right there until morning. I'm sure he will wake us all up. Bet our neighbors won't like it too much, but that's tough luck.

12

Rabbits Like Country Music

I don't know if I mentioned that the rabbits like music. I was singing to some country music and they could

hear me. They all sat there with their ears up and were looking at me in the window. It's funny to see. They must have pretty good ears because I'm inside the window. I am going to go out on the deck and sing to them there and see what they do then. I hope I don't scare the rooster away, ha-ha! I want them to get used to it here and music is part of our lives and they need entertainment just like all of us. I believe that music lifts the spirit and takes awat depression, if it's merry. Im sure rabbits feel like we feel..

13

🐇

OTHER ANIMALS THAT COME INTO OUR YARD

Last night we had a visitor. The biggest raccoon caught in our cage trap behind the fence. He was a nice and calm one. It didn't seem like it bothered himto be caught in there... Of course, we turned him loose by the pond. We don't want to hurt him. The pond has now, 29 possums and 14 raccoons all that we put there from here. We live on Panama City Beach in Florida and we don't where all these animals are comming from. One day, a few years back, a deer (buck) ran across our front yard and almost knocked me down. It was shocking, I was really amazed and stunned!

14

Busy Rabbits And Others

Today, we caught all the new babies that were in the yard and put them in the cages, all but one left we can't seem to get. He is way smarter than us and faster...

We are going to go to the Flea market again in Dothan and see if we can get a female hen to be with Rudy and look for rabbits as well. We plan to go to Troy again to Jimmy's for a big huge rabbit (female) for Kevin our neighbor. He has the male already. I'd like to get a few maybe. We don't need any more males, though. We will see how we feel. We may just go to Dothan.

One day my husband came in the house and said that the rabbits had eaten all his oleander plants that he had just planted and that they leveled them straight across. They tell us that those plants are poisonous, but the rabbits are eating

them all the time and we haven't had a death from them

When I went out to look, they were leveled like stubs, they are lucky they didn't get their little butts spanked..

Have you ever watched a rabbit for awhile, he will stand straight up and he looks like a little beggar. Some of our rabbits that are the older ones, come and eat out of our hand. Cinny, our oldest one, comes up on the porch ever day and we can feed her. She knows who she belongs to.

We see our squirrel who stays in our trees back there is now going on top of the rabbit cages like he's on his daily route. We have been putting nuts in the bird feeder now and he goes there now. You would say it is like the zoo, here...

When Rootbeer starts fighting and chasing the rabbits, I tap a certain way on the window and say, "Rootbeer," and he hears it and stops. He knows it is me and I mean to stop it.

15

Rabbits Come Home And More Stories

Some of the people who buy our rabbits, have little kids that get all excited when they come here to see them. They all want one each of their own. We've gotten around three back because of different reasons. One family was moving away to Texas and didn't want to take it there, another one said her little girl didn't play with it anymore, and the other one said she didn't want to clean up after the rabbit... You need to give them attention and put food and water in their dishes and clean up, but give love too, to have a rabbit. I have to give my husband credit for feeding them and water. I am really lax in that. I need to take more initiative... We take the rabbits back, though, because we want to and if you got 1 or 30 it is almost the same because you still have to put food and water out....

One of our good neighbors that used to live next door, was talking to my husband and he told him that he was afraid to let his dog go because he said he thought his little dog would chase the rabbit and catch it. My husband told him that it wouldn't happen and to let go of the dog. He let go and the dog shot after that rabbit and the rabbit let the dirt fly with his back legs and almost blinded the dog. He was gone like a shot, almost 2-3 times faster than the little dog.

16

🐇

WHEN BIG RABBITS WERE BABIES

When our big rabbits were small and babies themselves, we used to put toys in the cage and they liked them.. We had a truck they liked to sit on and one was behind the steering wheel and it was as cute as could be. We have pictures of it. One time we had a board up in the air in their cage and it went across the pen and you could see 6-7 rabbits in a row on it. It looked like an assembly line or they were having a town meeting. Ha! Ha! We also had a toy doll house and a barn they liked to go in and lay in. They also liked the toy corvette. We watched them in the drivers seat and took pictures because it was so hilarious.

One day we came home and my son Kevin had one baby bunny in the house and they were playing with him and pet him and he got pretty tame. That was "Rootbeer.

He is spoiled by us. He is now the bossy one, the stud mcmuffin of the bunch and understands us very well. Kevin liked to let him walk on him when he was lying on the sofa. That rabbit was held alot by Kevin and it got alot of love and attention by all of us. Kevin is paying alot of attention now to the baby in the pen called, Lollypop. She is a pretty little bunny with lop ears and comes up to the pen to greet everyone now, since she gave her so much attention. It really shows a change in a rabbit when they get love and attention. When I first went to see Lollypop, she would run away and so does Licorice, but maybe Licorice will come around when she gets more attention, too. Once you see these adorable bunnies you can't refuse them anything. They are so cute they wear on your heart…out of town, Kevin and Kevin are the rabbit sitters. They love them and take care of them while we are away……

17

🐰

New Rabbits And Hen

Saturday, we went to Dothan, again, to the flea market and Sue, the other lady we buy rabbits from was there. We were looking at the hens and ducks and when we started walking around her tent, mu husband said, "Oh no." I looked and there they were, 4 baby lionsheads and 3 of them were white and looked like Angel, the other one was a grayish-brown. Angel, was the white lions-head I lost only she was a tad bit bigger. These are babies, yet, I told Bob - we have to get them and take them home. I said' "Look how ADORABLE THEY are !" So, we asked Sue and she gave us a good deal on them and we got a hen from her too. We went home, unpacked our shopping bags, Bob clipped the hens wings so she can not fly away called her Bootie, took the new bunnies out to clean their new cage we bought today that goes in the house, put them in, I played with two of them for awhile and we fed everyone before bedtime and shower time. We did stop on the way home, I forgot, we bought a big white rabbit from a man named Joe at his house. We also bought a real nice cage for indoors for the little ones.We put the big whitw one in the big cage with the other bunnies outdoors and she likes it there with them. She is like a mother herself and keeps a watch on them.

18

RUDY AND BOOTIE

I woke up early this morning with the sound of Rudy, cockadoing and he still is not loud. Maybe, that's a good thing.

Bootie, the new hen, gets along great with him. They go walking, or should I say strutting around the back yard when we let them go during the day. They are really very nice animals. I haven't seen Rootbeer or Blondie, chasing them anymore. I think they are used to them now.

By the way, after Bootie and Rudy were put away last night Booties first night here, I found an egg on the ground, she laid there. I put it in her hay in the cage and Bob said she was laying on it this morning when he went to leave them out. That was quick, hey? I talked to Sandi at the feed store and she said it was the wrong time of the season, so to go gather the egg up and eat it. I never went to do that yet.

It seems like the rabbits and chickens are going to get along just fine. I don't see any fighting among them....

19

TALLAHASSEE TRIP, SUNDAY NO RABBITS

We are on the go all the time lately to flea markets. We went to Tallahassee flea market today, (Sunday,) and there wasn't a rabbit there at all. They probably brought their rabbits, yesterday (Saturday). That is usually the best day to go to the flea market, it seems like there is alot more animals on that day. I think we were blessed on Saturday, as well. We got alot of animals and the most special rabbits there is. We got them 4 for $50.00, and when they get bigger (they won't get real big) they are worth $35.00, or more, each. That's because they are rare and such a special breed from Belgium. We are going to have to look and see who is who and see which white one is the male. I want to put a color of blue on the male and nothing on Angel, a color of pink on the other white one and nothing on the grayish-brown one because we won't need to. I have named 1 white one, Angel, one white one Fifi, the male white one, Zee Zee, and the brown one, Gigi. These little bunnies look like angels. They sure are a gift from God. If this is what heaven has to offer, I sure want to be sure and get there...

20

Playing With Bunnies

It's a lot of fun to play with the bunnies. I pet them and let them walk around me on the sofa. When you pick them up you need to pull them in close to your chest because they sometimes like to squirm around. Last night when picked up Gigi (the gray-brown one) she was pretty good, but when I took one of the white ones she was squirming trying to get away and scratched me up, but sometimes they do. They are a little afraid when they are new and don't know you yet. These lion-sheads are so fluffy and soft. We gave the 4 of them a bath and they cleaner now. I don't want them to stink in my house. I'm sort of fussy about that. Right now I am watching them as I write and there are 2 kissing, so I assume one is the boy... It is really sweet! These two always huddle together and sleep together like that. The other two usually go by themselves. They must be quadruplets because they all look alike, even the grayish brown one. Tonight, I will take out one at a time before I work on typing my book. They need love and to get to know me. They had some grapes to eat and a few pieces of cabbage, plus the pellets and corn. We used to over feed the rabbits. It isn't good to do.

I believe that adults and children would love to read this title as they would like to hear and learn of all the experiences someone has had with rabbits or other animals and what they went through with these animals while they bred them.

21

Rudy And Bootie #2

We were sitting here eating supper, when all of a sudden we heard this loud noise,.. We listened again and figured it was Rudy screaming. He had gotten up on my table on the back deck and was hollering so loud and so long we thought he was hurt. Bob opened the back door and he was there still hollering and screaming. He kept looking at him and hollering until Bob was going to pick him up to put him back in his pen, and he jumped through the deck boards and walked over by his house. He looked at his house and went in. Then Bootie looked at it too and she jumped in the house. So, Bob locked up the coop. It was amazing to see that happen. We sure got a laugh out of that one. It is like he wanted to go in his pen but he wanted us to know that he needed the door locked behind them. Then he shut up and we haven't heard from him since tonight.. We wish the rabbits would do something like that, but that won't happen. They will run away instead..

22

Little Bunnies

The little bunnies we find like to go to the bathroom in their food dishes as they are eating. They will sit there in the bowls and eat their food and leave the mess and then the food is no good anymore, either. We don't like that so Bob took their dish and put a strap across the dish so they can't sit there anymore- they have to stay out and eat the right way now. So, if you have that problem, you know what to do, it works. They won't eat their food with poop on it , even though they did the damages- so we got tired of wasting food. You can get a plastic , round dish and put a big pipe in the middle of the dish, You can use an L shaped bracket on each side of the pipe and screw it to the bottom of the dish plastic, or whatever your'e going to use. It seems like all of the little ones have done that, so that is always our cure. They don't know that it isn't good to do, they have to learn, like us, what's right or wrong...See my illustration below for the dishes you can make......

23

Rudy's Attack On Me

It was a beautiful day, I was out back getting food and water for the animals. I went to put the food in the cage for the little bunnies and when I started back to the porch, I saw Rudy and Bootie comming towards me, only Rudy was comming at me real fast and I didn't have time to do anything and he bit my shin and I threw a fit at him. I don't know what happened. I don't know if it was the blue bowl I had in my hand going into the bunny pen, or what.. I've gotten along with Rudy until that day. I wish I knew what caused the attack- cause it shocked me and his peck broke my skin. The rabbits never have done that to me. Now, I take the hose with me to go back there because when I spray him, he knows to stop.. If he does it again, he's gone.. I won't put up with it, I've got too many animals to care for and he can't hurt anyone.... I won't even want to own an animal like that..

I'm scared of dogs. There are only a few that I'm okay with. I was bitten when I was a young teenager and now it stays with me since. Rudy's attack reminded me of the dog attack, so, yes, I was scared a bit, I can't say I don't like dogs, because I do, I'm just very leery of them now. I really do like animals pretty much.

Anyway, we will keep an eye on Rudy and see how it goes...

24

🐰

New Lionshead Bunnies Go Out In The Pen With The Other Babies

Tommorrow, we will be arranging the pen and we will putting the Lionshead babies with the other babies. The Lionshead babies need to get and be with the other babies. They also need to be able to move around more because the cage out there is a lot bigger and longer. It gets too messy in the house after a while, makes extra cleaning work. They look like they want to be out there with the others now , anyway. They want to run some so they will be able to more in that cage.

We put them in the cage with the others now and it seems like everything is going okay. One of our new, big, white rabbits (female) is in there with them now and she does well with them. The Lionshead babies have been drinking from the

Dottle of water on the cage, but I also keep a bowl of water in the cages. I guess they will get used to the big cage like the others. I was thinking about bringing them to Walmart and show my friends their at work, but I don't want to get kicked out for having rabbits in the store. Ha! Ha! I might do that one night when my friends go on break. They will be surprised what a Lionshead looks like. Everyone around that store seems to like animals.

25

🐰

KEVIN, MICHELLE, CHICK-FILET, 2, MARBLE AND SNOWBALL

When we went to Dothan that Saturday, we got the Lionsheads **and Bootie,** we got the white and black spotted rabbit for Kevin and Michelle down the street. They used to have Chick - Filet 1 and something happened to it so now they have this one we picked up and they call it Chick- Filet 2. We picked them up a big white one too, they call it Snowball. Then, I thought maybe would like one of the little marble ones we have from Rootbeer, and they call it Marble.. The rabbits look like a marble, too.. Chick Filet is a good name for that rabbit too, they remind you of the pictures you see of the cow colors, black and white.... All the rabbits are nice..

They have new cages that Kevin made for them too, and he also did a nice job. Kevin is a lot like Bob, they keep busy and really do an awful lot for these rabbits... Lucky rabbits! They are like our babies to us all, now, since our kids grew up. Michelle used to bring our bunnies lettuce, apples, and whatever was being thrown out at work. It sure helped a lot, none of those foods are cheap anymore,

Now, they keep the rabbits outside in their new pens. Rabbits do make a lot of mess in your house, so you might want to get a cage (put it up in the air, off the ground), made for outdoors...

26

BOB

My husband Bob, is really good to these rabbits.....He gets up early and he feeds them all, (most of the time.) He does this all before he does his other jobs around here... When Cinny is out front, he always makes sure she gets her food. She comes and begs, and he's right there to feed her. There is a little gray and white one, we need to catch and put in the cage. It comes with Cinny, it's a male... Yes, Bob really puts me to shame, because he does a lot more for the rabbits than I do, and I a, actually the one who wanted them. When I get up, everything id done, but I have a hard time going to sleep at night. There are times I stay awake 2 nights and days without sleep. He really treats them like they are all our kids. He treats our kids that wat, too.... These rabbits are all lucky around here. They have owners that love them, feed and water them, and whatever. Bob, makes the rabbits beautiful cages, and he has one he made that has a little house for the mothers to have their babies in. He divides them off, too, when they need to be apart for babies. There isn't much that Bob doesn't do for our little buddies....

27

🐰

STANDING UP TALKING TO EACH OTHER

Did you ever see a rabbit stand straight up on his hind legs? That is something you need to see. They are so cute and look so funny. They look as if they are begging for something. I don't really know why they do that, unless they want food or it may mean danger. I really believe that the rabbits talk to each other. They seem to warn each other when their is danger, we have seen that happen when a predator come in the yard. It's like they tell each other to beware. You will then see them facing all one way and not moving. It tells us too... Then we know that there may be a problem comming...

Remember, rabbits are the first on the food chain. Predators can smell rabbits for a long way off. All I know, is that when trouble is near, they must talk to each other. When you go with a net, I notice that it seems one is trying to tell the other one to run, they're comming with their nets...

28

🐰

JAKE AND JACKIE HAVE NEW ARRIVALS

Bob called for me to come out back, yesterday morning.. It was Jackie, our big black and white spotted female lop-ear. Her and Jake had babies. I don't know exactly how many she has, maybe 3-4. You have to watch because she has to know your scent or they may kill them or the father may. Bob says they are real chubby, like jackie and Jake. Bet they are cute as buttons... We pray she takes care of them or I will be bottle feeding again. You have to bottle feed them, if she doesn't feed them, or they will die without milk. If I have to be pushy with them to drink, I will. I don't want to lose any of them, if possible...These will be white babies with black spots and maybe little mustaches. They will also probably lop ears because the parents are both lops. I'm guessing they will be New Zealand lops... It is still hard to see them as they are still fur skin, before long they will be all furry and you will see what they are going to look like. It is sometimes hard to tell their sex when they are babies, but some people can tell....

29

🐰

MY OBSERVATIONS

You have to remember that what I am writing here in my book, are from our experiences we have had with our rabbits, and the hen and rooster, as well…... So, what I tell you has happened to us.

Rabbits are a joy to be treasured from God. It's just ashamed that their are so many predators out there to kill them. When you see a baby rabbit, there is nothing quite as precious. You fall in love with them. They are sosoft and cuddlely to hold and they will melt your heart. Even when they grow up, they are still the most dearest pet you'll ever see.

There have been a few people who have asked for meat rabbits, and I know exactly what they want. I tell them I don't sell any rabbits to eat they are all our pets, and I only sell them for such.

I have 3- that are meat eating rabbits, but they won't get hem. I don't believe in that, rabbits have a hard enough time just to survive. I hope you are enjoying my book…It is heart-felt and I try to tell you the things we've experienced and hope it will help you. I hope some of the things you've learned about will stay with you if you decide to have rabbits. I hope some of the bad things won't happen but some of these things I tell you, I hope helps

30

Bootie Lays Eggs

there must have been 7-8 eggs laying there from Bootie, each day a few more here and there. Did you ever eat hen eggs? They are the best, freshest eggs you ever want to eat......We ate Booties eggs and the eggs from the store and actually liked her fresh eggs better. It is pretty nice to get free eggs at the back door. Ha! Ha! I was a little scared to eat them at first, but they were sure great! She's been a pretty good hen around the yard. I saw her head towards one of the rabbits today, but she didn't do anything.......

31

Some Other Predators To Beware of

There are a few more predators to be aware of, although there are probably many more that I am unaware of. The owl, the fox, and the hawk, are among the predators we see around. We have seen fox around the area, we have seen the hawk out back on a tree on the property beyond our fence, and we see the owl in a tree as well. One day we found a bunch of feathers from the pigeons that come here on the hill to eat.. We don't know, but we think the hawk swooped down and got him. We saw all the feathers, but no body anywhere. I don't believe it was a rat, I believe the bird got swooped up after the feathers came off. That is just my guess, my opinion.. This happened in broad daylight.

One of the worst of all though, is the cat. They are like a vulture. They are very powerful and can do the most damage. I know you may think I am crazy, but believe me it is very true. This is why we say to have good wiring on your cage and be up off the ground. Remember that raccoons can also turn a lock on the cage. They are very clever creatures...

32

CINNY, AN INDEPENDENT FEMALE

Today, I was going out the door to go to the store and there was cinny, at my feet begging for food. I opened the car door and then couldn't leave because I knew she was hungry and needed food, so I went back in the house and got her some bread and crackers. She loves to eat and bread and crackers are a real treat to her. I went to feed her and she took it from me and ran a few feet away as if she was afraid someone was going to steal her food. She is like a little dog who wants you give her food. If you don't give her anything, she will follow you all over. She is one of the best baby producers here too, but she has been going over by the neighbors house to stay because when she had babies here last, they were all being eaten by something, maybe the cat and also the other rabbits kept bothering her too. She knows us really good because she is one of the first rabbits we had a long time and we can feed her by hand. She doesn't like us petting her anymore, she was only okay with that when she was small. It is funny how rabbits sometimes love to be pet and then they don't, they run... There are times when they let you pet them to get to know you, then the next time they see you, they know who you are and it's okay.. You can tell when Cinny comes to the front door, though what she wants. Usually, rabbits won't do that, but she is like a little human lady...

33

RABBITS DURING HURRICANES

The one thing we haven't mentioned is what do we do with the rabbits when a hurricane is comming. W e try to gather up all the loose rabbits that we see running on the ground, and hope we can catch them all with the net. Then, we have to find cages to put them in. After that they are all transported into our garage and there they are given all the food and drinks we can put before we leave. We have to keep them in there because that seems like the best place for them. It gets too windy back there and with too much of a strong wind a tree could fall on the cages, or the cages may get blown over or destroyed. There would be no use to try to carry 30 rabbits somewhere and leave them in a car. We took our dog we used to have with us the first few years we were here and hurricane 0 pal hit and we went to a shelter in Monticello, Florida up by Tallahassee and no dogs could go in, so we had to leave him in the car and we felt bad.. I worried about him all night, wondering if he was okay outside there. It would be really crazy to try to drag 30 rabbits with us to sit in a car. So, that's the way we go when a hurricane comes. Sometimes, we don't ever leave here, but if it seems real bad, we we have to because we live in a mobile home, and they may be dangerous to stay in near water. You just have to use your own judgement and come up with something that will suit your ways.

34

SILVER AND BRAINY CAUGHT. PRETTY
BREEDS

I went shopping today for Christmas and when I got home I was looking out at the little bunnies in the cage and I asked Bob who was in the cage because I knew that part of the cage had been empty and now there were two rabbits in there, but I was too far away to see who they were. Bob said he had caught the pretty silver colored one. It's a real beautiful lionshead that is a baby male to our Sammy, that's over the neighbors and he finally caught it. Then he told me he caught the little marble (female) one in a pipe. We call that "Brainy." We could never catch that one that is why we called her that. That is terrific- we are finally collecting all of our rabbits whom I have been missing... I want to get Sammy back too, she is real pretty, too, she breeds good now. She would make real wild looking babies if she bred **with** Rootbeer. Bob told me that Brainy and Silver don't get along in the pen, so he put brainy in with the other babies. Im betting if Rootbeer and Sammy bred together they would have gray, white, brown and silver markings. You wouldn't believe some of the colors you get from all the different rabbits

Sammy, is a lionshead but Rootbeer is a rex rabbit, I believe. Sonny, our lionshead is the son of the big Sonny we used to have. There are so many options of breeds, it's unbelieveable. You always end up amazed at what comes out in the end. It's usually some awesome babies you fall in love with. I can remember one rabbit that came out and it ended up looking like a little peanut.

She had a little girl face, and was pretty different than the others...

35

Sonny, Nosey, And Bootie Hen

Today, Bob said that Bootie, our hen, laid another egg... She lays around an egg a day it seems like.

Then he mentioned that the other day, Nosey, our black lionshead with the little white nose, was sitting out there watching him work. He said he just kept watching him for the longest time and he looked at him as if to say, "What are you doing?" "You're doing a good job." Ha! Ha! Nosey is like a triplet. The other ones are "Southpaw" who is black and has one left white paw. which is why I call him that. The other one has 2 white paws and a few other white markings, I call him, "Two-paws" The plain black one I call "Blackie." She is a female from a different family. She's not a triplet.

Now, let me tell you about Sonny. Bob told me that Sonny ran outside the fence because it was open the other day and Bob peeked around the corner and then he threw a rock and hit the fence and he said Sonny came running back inside the fence real quick. He probably got scared and ran in. Sonny is the lionshead son of Sonny and Cher. He's a sweet bunny, but some of the bunnies pick on him and he picks back. I hope I don't see any more of the picking cause I think Sonny is cool!

36

Nikki And Joe's Rabbit

My daughter, Nikki upton and her husband Joe, used to live here and one night we happened to go over to visit them and we saw her new rabbit she brought home. He looked like a real nice, pretty rabbit and he seemed like he was pretty healthy.. Well, she had boughten a rubber-maid container for him to stay in but come to find out that it wasn't good to do because the rabbit died. She called and told me he was just laying there dead and couldn't figure out what happened, or what killed him.. She said she called and talked to the pet store and they asked her if she had the rabbit by any plastic at all, and she told them that she had bought a plastic container for him to stay in. They told her that he died from the toxic that the container *inas* The plastic is toxic if they stay in it.

Who would ever think that would happen? That is another lesson that you and I both learned, because I was surprised to hear that. I would never had thought that. I guess Nikki and Joe had to bury the poor rabbit and I'm sure it made them feel bad, too. It would have made a nice pet. They have a sweet little dog, I like so much, and they had a cat at the time, so a rabbit was pretty neat too.

37

🐰

ROBBY LIKED THUMPER KEVIN LIKED SNOW BALL ANDERSON

When my oldest son, Rob got home from college in Tallahassee and was ready to move toPensacola he was here one week end when Thumper 2. was alive but had her tilt head disease. He doesn't seem to care for the rabbits, but when he was a little boy he had a rabbit and he called him Thumper, and his younger brother had a white rabbit he called Snowball Anderson. We never found out why he called it Andersn.

Anyway, Robby seemed to take a liking to poor Thumper 2 we had here. He pet it and carried it around a little, maybe he felt bad , I don't know, but when he found out later how such a tragic death Thumper had from a cat, he really got upset about it, He felt bad for Thumper.

Kevin, also had an experience when he was little, too, when SNOW-ball Anderson died, he buried her on Michigan Avenue in Panama City. We lived on Michigan Crt, in town when we first moved here. Then we didn't get any rabbits until after the kids were older and now they are gone and we have 20-30 rabbits like they were our kids.

38

🐰

SELLING RABBITS AND GIVING RABBITS

I haven't sold a rabbit for a while now. I took the sign down last summer and there weren't many left but those we were planning to keep. When we do sell the rabbits, they are $10.00 each, and it doesn't matter if they are big or small. I charge the same for all. I won't sell any of my lionsheads, though, if I decide to ever sell them, they will be a lot more.... Sometimes, when we are selling them, some people are poor, and when you talk to them you can pretty much feel if they will take of them because that is my concern. If they are in a pinch for cash, I WILL GIVE THEM ONI. I hope these people know that if they can't care for them, to please bring them back to us.. There are a lot of people who come here and then realize that they will need a cage, they need food, and you are faced with providing all the things they need to live. When they think for awhile, they sometimes decide not to enter into it. I rather they be honest because it is a chore and an expense…

39

ROOTBEER

I'll always remember the one special day we went to Dothan for rabbits, and we got Rootbeer. He was a tiny one, but he had bigger ears, but he was just as sweet as could be. I remember the trip home, I held him pretty much of the way home and pet him and loved him so much. He was an absolute joy from heaven. His brown eyes and his brown and white markings made hin a gift to me. I thought, how could something so precious end up in my arms. Well, he's been pretty spoiled here. Between Kevin, my son, and his girlfriend Jenna, and me, he got the most attenta ion than most of the rabbits. Now, he runs the show. He bosses all the others around, but he still is a gorgeous rabbit.. There is still a special bond between Rootbeer and me. He understands me and I understand him pretty much. I let him know, though, when he does something wrong. He knows the tap on the window. He knows by my tone of voice, too, if he needs to quit. Rabbits love attention! They love everything, pretty much

40

🐰

The Ending

It is time for me to come to the end of my book. I hope you have read and understood what our rabbit experiences were and use them at sometime in your life, if you decide on rabbits at any time in your life.

I am sure I will be writing a second book later in life that will have more experiences that we shall encounter, but for now, I must tell you that I have really enjoyed writing this book and hope you will have learned a lot of different things I've mentioned. Our rabbits are telling you, "Thanks for reading about us and we wish you well."

www.ingramcontent.com/pod-product-compliance
Lightning Source LLC
Chambersburg PA
CBHW021302280526

45784CB00005B/2475